Original title:
Shimmering in the Sea

Copyright © 2025 Creative Arts Management OÜ
All rights reserved.

Author: Ryan Sterling
ISBN HARDBACK: 978-1-80587-291-7
ISBN PAPERBACK: 978-1-80587-761-5

Honeyed Glow of the Setting Sun

The sun dips low, a jam-filled drop,
Fish flip and flop, like they can't stop.
A crab wears shades, strutting with flair,
While seaweed dances, without a care.

Kids splash about, they giggle and splash,
Seagulls squawk loudly, hoping for trash.
In this golden hour, laughter takes flight,
As the waves serve up a funny delight.

Celestial Dancers upon the Water

Stars above twinkle, quite wiggly and bright,
The moon in a tutu, oh what a sight!
Jellyfish jive like they've got a groove,
While fishy friends join in, making a move.

A plankton ball spins, so classy and grand,
Bubbling with giggles, a jellybean band.
They twirl and they spin, oh what a scene,
On this dance floor of water, so merry and clean.

A Mosaic of Light on Liquid Canvas

Colors collide, it's a paint-splashing spree,
With dolphins who dive like they're free as can be.
A pirate's parrot squawks, "Look at me go!"
While the seaweed waves like a glittery show.

Clams snap their shells with a snappy little tune,
All under the gaze of a grinning, bright moon.
The ocean's a canvas, so ripe for delight,
Bringing chuckles and joy, all through the night.

Pearls of Radiance in Ocean's Embrace

Pearls pop up like gumballs on a spree,
Bubbles giggle, floating wild and free.
An octopus throws a confetti parade,
Inviting the fish for a lavish charade.

Sandcastles wobble, they teeter and sway,
With a crab wearing crowns, leading the way.
Starfish applaud with a tickle of glee,
As laughter erupts in the sparkling sea.

Ethereal Gleams at the Water's Edge

The fish wore sunglasses, so chic and bright,
Tails flapping gently, what a silly sight!
Seagulls with beaks full of chips for a spree,
Dancing in laughter, as playful as can be.

Waves rolled in rhythm, a giggling tide,
Shells telling jokes, oh what fun to bide!
Crabs tried to moonwalk, slipped here and there,
The beach is a circus, oh what a fair!

Sparkle in the Deep Abyss

Deep down below, where the fish don't care,
An octopus juggling, with whimsical flair!
Starfish in tutus, they twirl and they spin,
While clownfish chuckle, just waiting to win.

A seahorse in glasses, reads maps upside down,
Sailing through coral, pretending a crown.
With bubbles like laughter, they float and they twine,
In this wacky ocean, the humor's divine!

Nautical Jewels in Twilight's Grip

Twilight arrives, with a glimmering glow,
Mermaids tell stories that ebb and flow.
A dolphin flips out, with grace unconfined,
While seaweed shakes hands - it's one of a kind!

Waves are high-fiving, in gleeful delight,
The sun bows to crabs, as day turns to night.
A clam hosts the dance, with pearls as the prize,
Laughs echo softly, beneath starry skies.

Undercurrents of Glitter and Grace

In the drift of the tide, where antics unfold,
Eels tell tall tales, both funny and bold.
Each bubble a giggle, each splash gives a cheer,
As fish form a chorus, "We're winning this year!"

The plankton throw parties, all glinting and bright,
As turtles do limbo, with shells feeling light.
With laughter as currency, in depths of the blue,
The ocean's got humor, and it's shining through!

The Ocean's Treasure Beneath the Surface

Bubbles rise like party hats,
Fish wear coats, look like aristocrats.
Shells debate, who shines the best,
While crabs perform a funny jest.

Starfish strut in their bright attire,
Waves dance close, but never tire.
A clam sings off-key, loud and brave,
For laughter's found in every wave.

Seaweed giggles in the breeze,
Tickling toes with playful ease.
Octopuses play hide-and-seek,
While dolphins jump, so strong, so sleek.

A treasure chest with nothing real,
Just shiny rocks and an old wheel.
But laughter's worth far more, you see,
Like sunlit joy beneath the sea.

Dancing Lights of the Ebb and Flow

Jellyfish twirl in elegant cheer,
Wiggling bobbles, oh so near!
Lights are bouncing, a silly show,
The ocean glimmers with a glow.

Clownfish joke, they're always bright,
With painted cheeks and giggles light.
Waves roll in, a rhythmic thrum,
And sea slugs join, all jiggly, numb.

Barnacles with mustache flair,
Ask for tips on how to care.
"Stay sticky, friends!" they all shout out,
And pull a dance, without a doubt.

Seagulls laugh, they can't resist,
Telling tales on waves, a twist.
Bubbles pop with each new jest,
In this wet world, we're all impressed.

Shards of Bliss on the Water's Edge

Sunlit shards, oh what a sight,
Twittering gulls take off in flight.
Crabs come scuttling, quick and sly,
While kids splash in with a joyful cry.

Shells hold secrets of the deep,
While jellybeans, the fishy creep.
Dance of squids, a silly grace,
Making all the fish lose face.

A dolphin pranks with flips and spins,
Chasing waves, where joy begins.
Starfish line up for a selfie shot,
Laughing together, why not? Why not?

At the shore, a treasure hunt,
Finding laughter's the main front.
With salty smiles and sandy toes,
The fun here grows, and joy just flows.

Rainbow Fish and the Glittering Waters

Rainbow fish with glimmer bright,
Flashing colors in morning light.
He tells tales of mishaps grand,
Where scales get tangled, like a band.

Blues and greens join in for fun,
Making waves, they laugh and run.
Fishy giggles fill the blue,
Sprinkling joy in every hue.

Sea cucumbers, in a race,
Trip on rocks, but win with grace.
Shimmery friends gather 'round,
In this quirky sea, joy's found.

A giant wave comes crashing in,
Washing away all grumpy chin.
Together they dance in salty spray,
In a world where laughter leads the way.

Celestial Glows on Water's Palette

Bubbles pop like joyful tunes,
Splashing fish wear party balloons.
Seagulls dance on a wavy rug,
Whales join in, giving a big hug.

Tootsie rolls float like candy dreams,
Crabs wear glasses, or so it seems.
Stars on waves play hide and seek,
Are those dolphins? Let's take a peek!

The moon tickles the water's face,
While turtles moonwalk with grace.
Jellyfish glow like disco balls,
As ocean laughter fills the halls.

With every splash, a smile is found,
Who knew the sea could dance around?
Waves surf on jokes the tides convey,
In this fun aquatic cabaret!

Ethereal Maneuvers of Ocean's Gleam

Octopus did a funny twirl,
While seaweed danced in a whirl.
Clams snap shut, it's quite the show,
Who knew that shells could steal the glow?

Fish in tuxedos take a bow,
Sardines sparkling, look at them now!
Seashells giggle in the breeze,
As sea stars shimmy with such ease.

Mermaids laugh, they giggle and flip,
Bubbles gather for a tiny sip.
Crabs play cards, what are their stakes?
In the sea, everyone just bakes!

Tides roll in with a chuckling cheer,
Belly flops from a porpoise near.
With every wave, there's boundless glee,
In this liquid world of silly spree!

Flickers of Hope on Aquatic Canvas

Seashells whisper secrets untold,
The fish wear hats, it's quite bold.
Starfish wave like friends at play,
"Let's make this a fun-filled day!"

Dolphins prance, they're full of cheer,
With squeaky sounds that all can hear.
The seafoam giggles, what a sight,
As tides tickle the shores at night.

A crab navigates his treasure map,
Chasing waves with a happy clap.
Barnacles cheer from their cozy homes,
Dance parties on these ocean foams.

A sandcastle stands, quite a display,
Whimsical towers built in play.
Every splash and giggle takes flight,
This aquatic world is pure delight!

Starry Veils Adorn the Horizon

Waves are creatures, making a fuss,
While fish tell jokes on a crowded bus.
The conch shell's gossip travels far,
As moonbeams twinkle, 'What a star!'

Cranky crabs with their sideways stride,
Race the currents with joy and pride.
Squid juggle pearls like they're balloons,
What a sight under the silver moons!

Clowns of the sea with fins all aglow,
Reef parties where nobody's slow.
A lobster cracks jokes, living the dream,
While the sea jokes louder, it seems.

With every splash, a giggle takes wing,
Playful antics, the sea's favorite thing.
In this watery world, smiles expand,
Join the laughter, let the fun be grand!

Threads of Gold on Ocean's Loom

The fish in the sea wear their finest suits,
With scales like disco balls, they do their jigs.
The seaweed waltzes, swaying like fools,
While crabs throw a party, with shellfish gigs.

A dolphin slips by, with a wink and a grin,
He jokes with the seagulls, they cackle with glee.
The octopus dances, eight arms in a spin,
While jellyfish giggle, just drifting carefree.

Starfish try to tango, but fall on their backs,
The sea foam erupts in a bubbly cheer.
A clam tells a joke, and everyone cracks,
As the tides roll in, bringing laughter so near.

So join in the fun, take a dive in the blue,
The ocean's a circus, a sideshow delight!
Underwater chuckles will tickle you too,
In this watery world, you're sure to feel light.

Hues of Enchantment Upon the Liquid Stage

A mermaid with flair stars in the play,
Her scales are a riot of colors so bright.
The sea turtles clap in their own goofy way,
While fish do impressions that gleam in the light.

The giant squid juggles with shells in a line,
While the starfish provide the background score.
Anemones blush at the scenes so divine,
As sea cucumbers whistle, begging for more.

The crabs take a bow, and the oysters create,
A wave of applause that echoes so wide.
The sunbeams applaud, thinking it's fate,
That seashells and barnacles share in the ride.

With laughter and antics, this stage is a feast,
The ocean's a ballroom, with each fish in a whirl.
So come to the show, you'll be charmed at least,
By the colors and giggles in the deep swirly swirl.

A Tapestry Woven by Ocean's Light

The little fish giggle, in bubbles they swim,
Creating a tapestry, bright as a rose.
With wriggles and twirls, their dance won't be slim,
As they weave through the currents, in styles they chose.

The clownfish perform, in a slapstick routine,
While seaweed joins in, with a comedic sway.
The pufferfish laughs, he's quite the marine,
As the wave tickles seabeds, coming out to play.

Bubbles pop loudly, like fireworks near,
The seahorses trot in their funny old way.
With laughter and joy, not a worry, no fear,
The ocean's a canvas, brightening the gray.

So dive in with glee, let your worries take flight,
In this realm of delight, where the sea's full of cheer.
With antics and colors, oh, what a sight!
A merry adventure, where laughter is near.

Starlit Canvas of the Briny Blue

The moon winks at fish, they're having a ball,
As crabs play charades on the sandy old stage.
The starfish applaud, though they can't move at all,
In the dark, they just twinkle, casting a sage.

Octopi juggle, their arms in a twist,
While seagulls dive by for a laugh and a snack.
A clam friend just sighs, 'Oh what did I miss?'
And the sea urchins giggle, rolling on back.

A treasure chest winks, full of trinkets galore,
As curious otters are stealing the show.
The currents swirl laughter from the depths to the shore,
A comedy masterpiece, keeping spirits aglow.

So come dip your toes in this whimsical tide,
Where creatures of wonder bring joy with a laugh.
In a world that's delightfully silly and wide,
The ocean's a theater, a comical half!

Aurora of the Coastal Night

Bubbles float like balloons, it's quite a sight,
Crabs wear tiny hats, oh what a delight!
Seagulls jest around, making quite the fuss,
Fish in a conga line, join the circus bus.

Waves play tricks like a jester at sea,
A dolphin's wink ignites a giggle spree.
Starfish in sun hats lounge without a care,
While turtles try limbo, in pairs they dare.

Depths unveil a stage for the quirky crowd,
Octopuses dance, and oh, they dance loud!
Scallops clap their shells, they cheer with glee,
A treasure chest flips, "I'm the star, see me!"

As night reigns in full, the sea shimmers bright,
Underneath the waves, it's pure comic delight!
Everyone laughing, caught in the spree,
Where nonsense reigns supreme, it's just fishy glee!

Refractions of the Deep

In the depths where seaweed throws a bash,
Clownfish wear tuxedos, but don't make a splash.
Anemones giggle, their tickles abound,
While grouchy old sharks just swim around.

Bubbles bubbling up, they form a parade,
A crab in a top hat, not one bit afraid!
A sea turtle races, his shell painted bright,
Yelling silly tunes, oh what a night!

Squid pens a postcard, "Wish you could see,
The dance-fest that's happening, right here with me!"
Ripples of laughter, echoes so clear,
As clams sing off-key, "Come join us down here!"

With jellyfish waltzing, and eels doing flips,
Even rocks have a jig, swapping playful quips.
Each wave a comedian, rolling in fun,
Underwater jokes land, when training a pun!

Dancing Gems of Fluidity

Glittering sprats passing wild giggling jests,
With sea cucumbers wearing silly vests.
Blowing bubbles like trumpets, they sound a tune,
While squids in tuxedos serenade the moon.

Waves shaking hands, they've got moves and groves,
Seahorses partnered, dancing under coves.
A clam on the mic, "Ladies and gents,
Here's a joke so great, it's worth a few cents!"

Nudibranchs twirling, colors quite divine,
Remind us they're pro in this underwater line.
Coral reefs cheering, they thrive on this cheer,
As sea anemones join, "We're all family here!"

The ocean, a stage, for laughter and grace,
With fishy comedians, it's a wild place!
Where water's a meme, and fun's in the flow,
Together we giggle, as tides come and go!

The Sea's Twinkling Tapestry

In the splashy spray, the mermaids play tricks,
While bubble-blowers toss, making light-hearted picks.
Clowns of the ocean, with fins bright and keen,
Mirthful in motion, what a colorful scene!

Starfish on stilts put on a grand show,
As octopus jugglers steal the deep glo.
Sardines doing flips, they swim in a line,
Their sparkly scales dazzling, like jewels they shine!

Pufferfish puffed, trying to leap with flair,
"Look at my bounce!" they joyously declare.
Seals spin around, boisterous with their glee,
While hermit crabs gossip, sipping coral tea.

The wild waves laugh, a joyous refrain,
Their ripples inciting a playful campaign.
With every salt-kissed breeze, a jolly spree,
The sea fills our hearts with whimsy and glee!

A Mosaic of Reflections

Splashing waves laugh and tease,
Fish wear sunglasses with ease.
Jellyfish jump in a polka-dot show,
Seaweed dances, puts on a glow.

Crabs in tuxedos scuttle about,
Doing the cha-cha, with a flout!
Shells wear hats, it's quite the spree,
Underwater parties, oh so free!

A dolphin jokes with a great big smile,
"Why swim alone when you can go in style?"
Starfish play cards, what a delight,
The ocean is lively, a colorful sight!

Mermaids giggle, they can't catch a break,
With octopus arm wrestles, make no mistake!
Bubbles rise, wrapped in cheer,
In this sea circus, you'll find good cheer.

Serene Twinkles in Blue Depths

Turtles in shades throne on the sand,
Planning a concert, isn't it grand?
Seahorses strum on kelp with flair,
Composing a symphony, beyond compare.

A school of fish forms a conga line,
Flipping and flopping, oh so divine!
While angelfish paint, colors collide,
Their art's so bright, it can't be denied.

A clam holds the spotlight with glee,
At the coral reef's talent jamboree.
With a wink and a nod, it takes the stage,
Reciting sea sonnets, setting the gauge!

As sea cucumbers do the macarena,
The ocean shimmies, like a ballerina.
Driftwood claps to the rhythm so neat,
In this underwater dance, life is sweet.

Chasing Silvers under the Moon

Moonbeams giggle, casting a chase,
Fish playing tag in the starry space.
"Catch me if you can!" they tease and glide,
Riding the waves on a playful tide.

Whales hum tunes that tickle the night,
Telling tales of their epic flight.
Barnacles gossip on a rock about fate,
As crabs engage in a crabby debate.

Squid ink a story with swirling flair,
Painting the waters—what a colorful affair!
A jellyfish leads with its glow so bright,
Creating a spectacle that fills with delight.

Sailor's delight at the treasure below,
As fish throw confetti, putting on a show.
Under the moon, laughter flows free,
This ocean party, as fun as can be!

Luminescence in the Aquatic Embrace

In a cozy nook of the ocean's warm chest,
Creatures gather, feeling quite blessed.
Anemones fluff, sprucing the place,
While mackerel giggles, wearing a face.

Parrots with feathers, oh so bright,
Tell jokes to the pufferfish every night.
"Why don't fish get ever lost?" they clap,
"Because they always follow the current map!"

A zany stingray drags in a snooze,
Distracted by the whirl of the hues.
Nudibranchs waltz in a colorful trance,
Twisting and swirling, giving a chance.

At the sea floor ball, laughter ignites,
As otters juggle clams, oh what sights!
Together they twirl in aquatic embrace,
Creating a carnival in this wondrous place.

The Celestial Dance of the Water Spirits

Bubbles bounce like jumping beans,
Underwater giggles, what a scene!
Fish in tuxedos twirl and prance,
Crabs do the cha-cha, taking a chance.

Jellyfish glow like disco lights,
Kicking up waves in silly fights.
Starfish show off, they can't resist,
In this ocean party, none are missed.

A clam takes a selfie, filters in play,
While octopuses juggle, oh what a display!
Turtles in sunglasses, chilling with flair,
In the deep blue fun, there's laughter to spare.

Mermaids crack jokes, it's quite the affair,
With dolphins that splash, they fill the air.
Under the surface, joy knows no bounds,
In the aquatic realm, pure laughter resounds.

Warm Hues Kissing the Ocean's Waves

Sunsets throw paint with a wink and a grin,
Colors collide, let the giggles begin.
Seagulls squawk silly, their wings a blur,
While seashells whisper of things that occur.

Crabs in the sunset do a little dance,
As sardines shimmer, they join in the prance.
A stingray glides with a flip and a flair,
Turning seaweed into a fashionable hair.

Tide pools are bustling with slapstick humor,
As barnacles argue, becoming a rumor.
Tiny fish tease with a wink and a splash,
Turning the twilight into a colorful bash.

With every wave, laughter flows free,
In this world of warmth, come swim with me.
Under the palette of reds and gold,
The ocean's cauldron of fun, we behold.

Ephemeral Glimmers of a Nautical Night

Stars in the water twinkle and laugh,
As ocean critters enjoy their own craft.
The moon plays peek-a-boo with a wink,
While shrimp serve punch with a side of pink.

Anglerfish flashing like disco balls,
They draw in guests to their midnight halls.
Grouchy old eels, they sulk and they frown,
While dolphins spin tales turning upsidedown.

The tides whisper secrets in echoes of light,
As clowns in the sea keep the party bright.
A seahorse rides in on a wave with a sigh,
Proclaiming, "Tonight, let's see who can fly!"

While crabs play cards with sea urchins around,
The jellyfish waltz, gliding without sound.
In this underwater gala, oh what a sight,
Where laughter's the key to the Nautical Night.

Ethereal Ebb of Colorful Dreams

In the depths of the blue, dreams take a dive,
With squids writing poems, oh how they thrive!
A rainbow fish shows off its glittery gleam,
While otters play tag in a slippery stream.

Waves tickle toes of sandcastles grand,
As seaplants whisper their secrets unplanned.
Turtles tell tales of their wanderlust,
While sharks munch popcorn, it's a huge must.

Frolicking feasts under starlit skies,
With starfish collecting the best of the fries.
As krill make confetti, oh what a scene,
The ocean's a carnival, bright and serene.

In this dreamy ebb, smiles fill the air,
Joy swims together without a care.
So come, take a dip in this vibrant stream,
And laugh with the creatures of color and dream.

Jewel Tone Currents

In the depths where the fish play,
They wear outfits, bright and gay.
An octopus in a top hat spins,
Sardines dance with silly grins.

Bright coral flashes like disco lights,
Crabs do the can-can, what funny sights!
Starfish are judges, holding a show,
With all their arms, they wave and say, "Go!"

A dolphin slides down a giant wave,
With jellyfish umbrellas, they misbehave.
The sea turtle says, "I'll race you all!"
But don't be late, or you might fall!

The seagulls squawk their quirky puns,
While a clam's like, "Hey, I'm just here for fun!"
Barnacles clap, though it's a bit slow,
In this wacky world beneath the flow.

Mirage of the Rippled Horizon

On the crest of each bouncing wave,
Fish sport sunglasses, cool and brave.
Seashells gossip, oh what a tease,
Crabby tales that weaken the knees!

A catfish juggles pearls on a dare,
While a clownfish goes, "I don't care!"
The horizon twists, it giggles a bit,
As flounders shout, "We're all having a fit!"

Mermaids laugh, with glittering tails,
While sea cucumbers tell their tales.
"Wait for me!" the shrimp says with glee,
When the tide rolls back, they all flee free!

Underwater, the antics won't stop,
A whale plays hopscotch—what a flop!
And when night falls, they still kick and sway,
In this mirage where laughter holds sway.

Crystalline Secrets of the Ocean

In the depths where secrets lie,
A crab sings low, a fish will fly.
Who knew a starfish could rap so loud?
With seaweed dancing, they draw a crowd.

Bubble-blowers blow bubbles so big,
As shrimp parade in a tiny pig wig.
The seahorse says, "Hey, join my game!"
As clams try to play, but feel quite lame!

Nemo's cousin is dressed like a king,
And sings about the joy that waves can bring.
Anemones sway like they're on parade,
While fish in tuxedos aren't at all afraid.

The octopus paints with colors so bright,
While turtles roll in a playful fight.
What secrets are whispered in water so deep?
Just let out a laugh, and take a leap!

Lighthouses Amongst the Stars

Under a sky full of fish-shaped stars,
Lighthouses giggle with lighted guitars.
They dance with the waves, what a beautiful view,
And each blink of a beacon brings laughter anew.

The crabs tap their pincers like it's a beat,
As seagulls get busy, on fish they will cheat.
"Who's the captain?" the flatfish will cry,
Reef parties erupt as bubbles go high!

A lobster juggles with sea urchin friends,
While hermit crabs debate on new trends.
"Wear a shell or go naked?" they ask the sea snails,
As laughter rolls on with the tides and the gales.

High above, where darkness meets light,
The lighthouses flash jokes that feel just right.
In this cosmic dance, they twinkle and twirl,
As the ocean joins in with a happy whirl!

Radiance in the Wake of the Tide

Fish in tuxedos dance around,
Making quite a splash with each bound.
Seagulls gossip, feathers in a twist,
Surfing on laughs that they can't resist.

Crabs wear shades, thinking they're cool,
Pinching their pals just to break the rule.
Starfish flip-flop, getting some sun,
Creating a ruckus, having their fun.

Surfboards floating, jellybeans sway,
Underwater parties every day.
A whale belly flops, causing a stir,
Splashing the crowd, what a big blur!

Octopus juggling, it's quite a sight,
Waving its arms, from left to right.
As fishy friends launch a great dive,
With giggles and glee, they're all so alive!

Waves Adorned in Diamonds' Touch

Mollusks with bling, strut down the line,
Glimmering colors that look so fine.
Barnacles gossip, all stuck in place,
While seaweed dances with floppy grace.

A dolphin in shades, surfing on foam,
Squeaking with joy, it feels like home.
The tide rolls in with tickles galore,
Bringing the laughter right to the shore.

Clams throw a party, sandcastles rise,
With splashes of laughter under bright skies.
Crabs on their back, waving their claws,
Poking each other with silly guffaws.

Seashells are clinking like they're at a bar,
Mixing sea drinks, it'll raise the bar.
The ocean's a stage, with wave after wave,
Where giggles abound and no one can save!

Brilliance between the Currents

Anemones giggle, tickled by tide,
Wiggling like they've got nothing to hide.
The schools of fish doing synchronized moves,
In jellybean patterns, everyone grooves.

A crab on a scooter, racing the wave,
Laughing and squeaking, oh how they rave.
"As fast as the tide!" he calls with a cheer,
While turtles are lounging, sipping their beer.

Dolphins show off with flips full of flair,
Sea horses sigh, "Do we really care?"
The ocean's a circus, the stage is so set,
With laughs and jests, a big fishy duet.

Oysters play cards, claiming they're wise,
While playful plankton throw pies at the skies.
The dance of the sea, it swirls with delight,
Where every laugh echoes through day and night!

Shining Paths on Tidal Shores

Seagulls in bowties pick up the pace,
Scavenging snacks at a lively place.
The barnacles gossip, all in a fuss,
While jellyfish float on a small school bus.

Sea cucumbers line up for the show,
With giggles and wiggles that start to grow.
The sand's their dance floor, the waves keep the beat,
As starfish do the limbo, oh what a feat!

A seal behind sunglasses, grinning so wide,
Rolling with laughter, it's all bonafide.
Tide pools are bubbling with bubbles of fun,
As the ocean gives birth to laughter, oh run!

Bubbles of joy, floating up high,
With laughter and splashes to light up the sky.
Each wave brings a chuckle, let's all take a dive,
For this sea of humor is blissfully alive!

The Dance of Light and Tide

The sun wears sunglasses, oh so cool,
While fish throw a party, that's the rule.
Crabs join the conga, dancing with flair,
Seaweed shakes it off without a care.

Seashells gossip, sharing their tales,
While dolphins giggle, flipping in trails.
A starfish takes selfies, 'look at my pose!'
The water's a dance floor, everyone glows.

A seagull joins in, with a laugh and a glide,
He trips on a wave, what a funny ride!
The tide rolls in, but no one takes heed,
For laughter and joy is all that we need.

As the sun sets low, the fun doesn't cease,
Octopuses juggle in a fit of peace.
With waves as our music, let's jump and cheer,
In this underwater club, we'll stay without fear.

Chromatic Currents Whispering Secrets

In a rainbow fish fin, secrets unfold,
A crab tells a joke, but it's a bit old.
The jellyfish giggle, drifting with grace,
While clams laugh so hard, they turn a bright pink face.

The currents swirl colors, blue, green, and red,
A turtle shows off his stylish new thread.
Whispers of laughter ripple through the brown sand,
As sea stars applaud with a wave of their hand.

Clownfish in tuxedos, dance with delight,
While bubbles blow kisses, soaring in flight.
A treasure chest opens, sharing its gold,
But what's really funny? It's just growing mold.

With sunbeams like disco lights, all around,
The ocean's a stage, laughter's the sound.
So join this parade of smiles and cheer,
For where there's humor, there's nothing to fear.

A Rainbow Lullaby to the Whispering Waves

The ocean hums softly, a sweet little tune,
With shells clapping hands, under the moon.
A fish dreams of flying, with wings oh so bright,
But wakes up to seaweed, much to its fright.

The snails slow dance, with moves quite bizarre,
While crabs throw confetti from under a star.
The waves start to giggle, tickling toes,
What a wild party, where laughter just flows.

A starfish sings softly, her voice full of glee,
While a group of sea cucumbers join in for free.
Seahorses cartwheel, with such silly grace,
Leaving trails of bubbles, all over the place.

In this lullaby, under starlit skies,
Everyone's welcome, bring your best guise.
So swing with the tides and let your heart sway,
In this joyful sea, let's dance all day.

Flickers and Wafts of Ocean's Lullaby

The waves share whispers, as they tumble and roll,
A crab steals the spotlight, playing the role.
Clownfish paint colors on a canvas of blue,
While sea foam chuckles, with a splash and a woo!

As starry rays twinkle, the sea laughs with light,
A dolphin does flips, what a marvelous sight!
Sea urchins play tickle, with spines sharp yet kind,
And conch shells snicker, their humor refined.

A walrus brings snacks, all piled in a heap,
But otters are giggling, they can't get to sleep.
The narrators are jellyfish, swaying like trees,
Telling wild tales that float with the breeze.

As twilight descends, the fun doesn't wane,
Laughter is painted on the ocean's own frame.
Join this buoyant ball, let your spirit roam free,
In the ocean of giggles, there's magic, you'll see!

Flickering Echoes of the Deep Blue

A fish in a tutu does a little dance,
While crabs on the floor give a sideways glance.
The octopus juggles with great delight,
While seaweed waves back, oh what a sight!

A dolphin in sunglasses swims by with glee,
Singing pop songs in perfect harmony.
With a splash and a flip, they steal the show,
The crowd of sea critters all cheer and glow.

Anemones gossip with clams on the sand,
Trading their secrets, all carefully planned.
A starfish multitasks, is that really true?
Serving sea snacks while it ties a shoe!

So here in this world where the waves jump and sway,
Creatures have fun in their own silly way.
In the depths of the blue, life's a humorous spree,
And laughter's the treasure—we all can see!

A Lullaby of Radiant Tides

The jellyfish drifts, wearing a nightcap,
While snails sing a tune, what a sleepy trap!
Seahorses yawn with their tails all entwined,
In this ocean bed, dreams are one of a kind.

Dolphins recite bedtime stories so bright,
To starfish who settle for a long, cozy night.
"Once upon a time," they begin with a grin,
Of mermaids who danced until the dawn would begin.

The bubbles arise and pop with soft glee,
Tickling the turtles who float endlessly.
"Did you hear the one?" says a crab in a shell,
As the tide cradles all in its soothing swell.

So drift away gently on this lullaby,
Where sea critters giggle and starlight passes by.
In the hush of the waves, dreams come out to play,
With laughter and joy that never fade away!

Soft Whispers of Dappled Light

The little clownfish paints with a brush,
Creating a mural amidst the coral rush.
While shrimp on parade do a wiggly jig,
Winning the prize for the best little gig!

Light dances down through the cerulean hue,
As the sea cucumbers join in the view.
A turtle in glasses, reading a book,
Says, "Let's be wise, take a better look!"

Goby fish swap tales in the sandy bright,
While sea sponges chuckle with pure delight.
"Oh, isn't it silly?" a dolphin erupt,
When an octopus' shorts simply won't stop!

With stars in the water and joy all around,
These curious creatures are humor unbound.
Laughter abounds in the depths of the night,
As they splash and they play in the soft dappled light!

Dimensional Dreams Between the Waves

In a realm where the seaweed has tales to weave,
A crab dreams of sailing, dreaming to leave.
With stars as its compass and fish as its crew,
They'd tackle the waves with a buoyant view!

The tiny shrimp float on rafts made of leaves,
While singing funny tunes that nobody believes.
A whale in a bowtie joins in for the fun,
Making waves from laughter, under the sun.

Flounders in flip-flops swim all around,
Competing for gigs with their antics profound.
A seagull debates with a talking shell,
Telling jokes that no one can truly tell!

So jump into depth where the weird meets the bright,
Adventures await in the clear moonlight.
In this silly world where the waves are your guides,
Every splash and each giggle, the ocean provides!

Illuminated Trails on Sandy Shores

The crabs in little suits dance in a line,
While seagulls squawk jokes, being quite divine.
Footprints vanish quickly, like secrets in sand,
As waves laugh at stories the beachcombers planned.

Drifting on jellyfish, the kids squeal with glee,
Trying to surf while yelling, "Look at me!"
But the tides are sarcastic, they pull and they tease,
While shells play peek-a-boo, hidden with ease.

Starfish hold conferences, all trying to lead,
Debating if groups should form quite a speed.
With flip-flop mishaps and sunscreen galore,
Each sunset marks laughter, who could ask for more?

As night blankets all, with a mischievous wink,
The moon spills its giggles, don't stop to think.
With each splash of foam, the shoreline will jest,
The ocean's just kidding, it's far from a test.

Moonlit Pilgrimage of Fleeting Lights

Bouncing beetles glow, like twinkling delight,
Chasing giddy shadows in the heart of the night.
The breeze tells a tale, with phrases absurd,
While fish flash their smiles, like they're part of the herd.

Crickets play tunes in the tall marshy grass,
As otters provide antics, quick as they pass.
Twilight trails blushing with laughter and cheer,
The stars join the dance, "We're brighter this year!"

With glowing nibbles, the snacks seem to float,
Like treasures unearthed from the old mariner's boat.
Each giggle from waves, a secret they keep,
As laughter rocks softly, lulling to sleep.

And though the night fades, with much left to share,
The sea still sings stories, for all who will dare.
In this watery gala, the lights twinkle free,
Reminding all wanderers, how fun it can be.

Glacial Glows in the Surf

Icicle popsicles float by with a grin,
While dolphins play poker, sure to reel you in.
The waves throw a party, all raucous and bright,
With penguins as judges, still ready to fight.

Snowflakes wear sunglasses, quite stylishly bold,
Each flake tells a story, as fun as it's told.
The surf's full of secrets, like dance routines,
While seals crack one-liners, with spotlights, like scenes.

The tide plays the jester, at every sharp turn,
With slippery moments, you'll laugh till you burn.
A riptide of giggles rolls in every time,
As walruses recite ancient funny rhyme.

And as day winks away, the sun starts to snooze,
You'll find that the surf has no time for the blues.
Each bubble, a chuckle, each splash, a delight,
In these glacial glows, the humor's just right.

Harmonies of the Deep's Luster

The fish band is jamming, with scales all aglow,
While octopuses clap in a synchronized show.
The seaweed sways gently, dancing along,
As turtles croon tunes, a water-nymph song.

Bubbles are laughter, rising high to the top,
While clams hold their breath, just waiting to plop.
Coral takes selfies, all colors and hues,
As snails wear the trendiest shells for their views.

The crabs tap their claws, keeping tempo so neat,
While shrimp do a shuffle, as they dance on the beat.
With harmony bubbling, all creatures unite,
An undersea concert, a whimsical sight.

As tides hum the chorus, a ripple of cheer,
The deep offers laughter, a treasure so dear.
In each wave's muddy whisper, a melody flows,
A deep-sea cabaret, where the fun always grows.

Cascade of Colors on Briny Tide

A fish in a tux, quite flashy and bold,
Swims with a swagger, might start a gold mold.
With each flip and twist, it's quite the charmer,
Waving its fins like a sub-aquatic farmer.

A crab in bright shades, painting the floor,
Dances like crazy, a real underwater chore.
Jellyfish jellybean, floatin' with glee,
Jumps into disco, let's join the spree!

Starfish auditioning for the next Broadway,
Sings to the waves, a fabulous display.
Coral reefs chuckle, it's a riotous scene,
As the sea boasts its most colorful sheen.

Glints of Magic in Ocean's Breath

A seahorse prances, with wishes galore,
While a clam plays the drums, what a bumpy score!
Crabs wear a crown, declaring a feast,
With shells on a platter, they're ready to be least.

Mermaids hold casts, casting spells on the sand,
This sea life party's simply unplanned.
Dolphins pop popcorn, that's quite the surprise,
As octopuses juggle, to everyone's eyes!

Turtles in shades, lounging so grand,
Claiming the rocks, it's their ticket to land.
A fishy fiasco, what's next on the list?
Join in the fun, it cannot be missed!

Whirls of Twinkle on Wave's Crest

Squids with their pens, writing poems by night,
Ink swirling in patterns, a dazzling sight.
Fishy folks giggle, a tickle they share,
With bubbles of laughter, from everywhere!

A puffin parades, in a feathered brigade,
Making quite ripples, to throw off a raid.
Lanternfish sparkle, like tiny bright stars,
Throwing a party, complete with guitars!

Walruses wobble, their dance like a dream,
Jelly blobbing along, like an innocent cream.
The sea plays its tunes, under moon's gossip,
The waves join the chorus, for a fun lil' trip!

Flickering Hues in Twilight's Grasp

Anemones waving, with whimsy and flair,
While shrimp hold a contest, for best hair-dare.
Eels in their finery, slipping with style,
Trade secrets of fashion, stay a while!

Clownfish in polka dots, do the cha-cha,
Hosting a party, let's dance on the plaza.
With crabs and their sass, they scuttle and sway,
In the twilight's amusement, they frolic away!

The moon winks at all, a bright little tease,
As barnacles chuckle, relishing the breeze.
With tales from the tides, absurd and sincere,
The humor of ocean's grandeur draws near!

The Winking Waters' Serenade

A crab in a tux, he takes the stage,
Dancing with fish from an ancient age.
The waves chuckle softly, their secrets they keep,
While a dolphin in glasses dives deep in a leap.

The seagulls wear hats, quite out of style,
Lobbing fish like footballs, all with a smile.
A hermit crab's hat, so hopelessly grand,
Is flung by a wave—like it wasn't well planned.

The shells gossip loudly, a conch leads the chat,
While octopuses twist in a rhythmic svelte spat.
The starfish applaud, though clapping's tough work,
They all think they're Glee Club—that's the quirk!

In the glow of the moon, they show off their flair,
Underwater limbo? You bet! They don't care.
With bubbles of laughter, it's quite the affair,
A seaside soirée, full of sea-witted dare.

Starlit Horizons and Ocean Dreams

The fish wear bow ties, elegant and neat,
Sipping on seaweed, quite the gourmet treat.
With winked eyes, they plot a grand buffet,
Spaghetti from kelp that has seen better days.

The lobsters hold court, all red and so proud,
Telling tales of giants—oh, they're quite loud!
With shrimp on the side, all dressed up for fun,
Performing a jig 'til the rising sun.

A whale plays the trumpet, what a sight to behold!
Making waves with the rhythm, it's pure rock-and-roll.
The mermaids all swoon, their hair a wild mess,
As the dolphin DJ spins tracks with finesse.

As quiet descends, they ponder their quests,
In search of lost treasure, that's a fun jest!
With dreams of a treasure that's shiny and bold,
They giggle in waves, as the stories unfold.

The Glint of Treasure Beneath

A treasure map made of seaweed and sun,
X marks the spot where the crabs had their fun.
But the gold turned to shells, what a quirky surprise,
Now everyone's dancing in makeshift disguise!

The octopus leader is lost in a trance,
Swaying to rhythms that make fish want to dance.
With pearls as their props, they put on a show,
As jellyfish turn lights for a blinky glow.

They dig and they dig, unearthing some junk,
A shoe and a bottle—now that's quite the hunk!
The laughter erupts like bubbles in foam,
As the mermaids break out in a seabed-style home.

With hearts made of laughter, they search for their gold,
Finding joy in the journey, more precious than old.
In the depths of the blue, they'll always agree,
Life's a funny treasure beneath the great sea!

A Tidal Symphony of Glows

Bubbles like notes in a sharp, lively tune,
Where clownfish perform under bright silver moon.
The seaweed sways gently, a soft, swirly beat,
While turtles join in with their flippery feet.

With rhythms so catchy, the dolphins unite,
Bouncing off waves, they take off in flight.
They leap through the spray, all giggles and glee,
While the starfish do cheer, as still as can be.

A parade of bright lanterns, the jellyfish glow,
Shining out brightly wherever they go.
The scallops click shells like castanets bright,
While the sea cucumbers wobble in fright!

In a tidal crescendo, they dance on the shore,
With laughter and joy, they can't take any more.
As night swallows light, they wave their goodbyes,
Resurfacing dreams with the rise of the skies.

Sparkling Reflections on Water's Skin

The fish wear hats, it's quite absurd,
They gossip about the passing bird.
With water glasses raised in cheer,
They toast to waves, let's party here!

A jellyfish's dance is quite the sight,
Electric moves that glow at night.
They twirl and swirl with playful grace,
A sea ballet in this aqua space!

Crabs in tuxedos scuttle around,
Tapping their claws to the ocean sound.
They hold a grand ball on the shore,
Inviting all, who could ask for more?

Seagulls squawk with a comedic flair,
Diving down low, but what do they dare?
A splash of fun, a squirt of sand,
This watery stage, how it looks so grand!

Dance of the Ocean's Light

Dancing rays in a playful suit,
Swim along to a tune so cute.
Barnacles keep the beat in time,
Their music soft, a gentle rhyme.

Turtles strut in a slow parade,
While dolphins demonstrate their trade.
With flips and jumps, they steal the scene,
An underwater circus, oh so keen!

Octopuses juggle driftwood and shells,
While starfish cheer with giggles and yells.
They flip their arms in raucous glee,
The ocean floor's a jubilee!

A sponge might sing, off-key but loud,
Enticing fish to join the crowd.
With bubbles rising to join the sound,
The ocean's humor knows no bound!

Radiant Depths Beneath the Skies

In pastel hues, the seaweed sways,
Fish play peekaboo in playful ways.
A clam sings tunes in a baritone,
While crabs roll their eyes, oh, what a drone!

Serenading corals, the sea fans sway,
While mermaids giggle, livin' the sway.
They toss seaweed like it's confetti,
A coastal party, the mood is ready!

Pufferfish puff, but it's just for fun,
A fashion statement under the sun.
They strut with flair, oh what a sight,
In this watery world, feel so light!

Starfish rise to take a bow,
They surely think they're quite the wow.
With every wave, a tickled laugh,
The ocean knows how to have a gaff!

Twinkling Dreams on Salted Surface

The salt-rimmed dreams bob and glide,
Pinching rays as they take a ride.
Seashells chat with a clever spin,
About the critters that once swam in!

The breeze tickles, a playful tease,
While plankton's pulling off a breeze.
They glow like stars in the evening tide,
In this salty realm, there's nothing to hide!

Whales crack jokes in deep water jokes,
While fish share laughs at their goofiness folks.
A comedy night, beneath the moonlight,
In this maritime theater, all feels just right!

A seagull winks with a cheeky flair,
Diving for snacks without a care.
And when they leave, the sea gives a sigh,
What funny antics just passed by!

The Radiant Embrace of the Marine World

In a circus of fish, they wriggle and sway,
Jellyfish dance in pajamas all day.
A crab with a top hat, oh what a sight,
Waves burst with laughter, oh what a night!

A whale's serenade with a kazoo in tow,
Surfboards are riding a jellyfish flow.
Octopuses juggle their hefty meals,
Each splash a tickle, the ocean reveals!

Starfish applaud from their sandy retreats,
While sea turtles tango, tapping their feet.
The dolphins are giggling, flipping with cheer,
The sea is our stage, let's bring on the beer!

So grab your snorkel and join in the fun,
With crabs and fish, we're second to none.
In this watery realm, we'll laugh till we pout,
For the finest of jokes, it's the tide that won't tout!

Tidal Reflections of a Distant Moon

The moon whispers softly, to the waves below,
They giggle and splash, in a moonlit show.
A seal in a tutu spins with pure glee,
While the starfish sit winking, oh how fishy!

A sardine sings songs about ancient lore,
To a clam who just can't take it anymore.
The seagulls are hecklers, cawing loud pleas,
Why does the saltwater taste like these cheese?

The tides pull and push, like a bad dance date,
As crabs slip and slide, oh isn't it great?
The night is alive with sea creatures that play,
Under a spotlight of moonbeams at bay!

So dive in with laughter, don't let it wane,
For the ocean's grand show is our sweetest gain.
With bubbles of joy, and a sprinkle of fun,
Under the moonlight, the night's just begun!

Liquid Echoes of Celestial Light

Far beneath the water, the glow worms ignite,
They play peek-a-boo, with bubbles in flight.
An anemone tickles a fish with a grin,
While barnacles chuckle, their patience wears thin.

As jellybeans jive, in a splendid parade,
The sea cucumbers dream of a pink masquerade.
A group of fine seahorses, elegant sprites,
Twirling in currents, in glittering lights.

The crabs play detective, with magnifying glass,
Searching for treasures, from the kelp they harass.
The tide rolls in laughter, a giggle bestowed,
As fishies hold hands in a whimsical load.

So let's dip our toes where the wiggly roam,
In the world of the deep, we've found our true home.
Where every wave whispers a joke or a tune,
In liquid reflections, let's dance with the moon!

Glow of the Horizon in Gentle Swell

On the edge of the ocean, where the sun wears a grin,
The seagulls play soccer, let's cheer for the win!
A dolphin in flip-flops is surfing in style,
With a banana boat crew that's gone for a while.

The waves have a secret, a ticklish delight,
As starfish throw parties under the moonlight.
The sandscript reveals a riddle or two,
A clam in a tux is inviting you too!

With narwhals in bow ties, they waltz on the tide,
While mermaids make bubbles, oh let's take that ride!
The laughter erupts, like a foam-covered crest,
In the glow of the horizon, we're all at our best!

So venture out far, where the funny fish dwell,
In the sea's merry theater, let's ring every bell.
With smiles and with giggles, and splashes of fun,
In the heart of the water, our laughter's begun!

The Enchantress of Glimmering Waters

A mermaid with a sparkling flair,
Dancing with fish, what a funny pair!
She juggles shells and sings a tune,
Tickling the crabs under the moon.

The seaweed waves like a silly hat,
As seahorses play chase, imagine that!
Octopus winks with his eight grand arms,
Saying, "Join us! We've got all the charms!"

Starfish giggle as they float around,
With silly faces, they can't be bound!
The waves clap hands; they can't get enough,
In this silly sea, it's all about fun!

If you swim close, you might just see,
A whale with glasses sipping sweet tea!
Every splash is a laugh to be heard,
Come dance with us, join the absurd!

A Symphony of Light Under Waves

Bubbles pop like tiny balloons,
Fish throw parties to jazzy tunes!
A lobster moonwalks, quite a sight,
The starry night's his stage tonight.

Jellyfish glow like disco lights,
Dancing merrily, oh what delights!
Clownfish play hide and seek in glee,
While corals cheer, "Look at me!"

Shrimps wave flags, they're tiny and proud,
Making a splash, singing out loud!
It's a carnival under the tide,
With sea critters dancing side by side!

Twinkling shells line the sandy floor,
As squids perform tricks, we all want more!
Laugh and wiggle in this ocean stage,
Each wave a joyous, playful page!

Mirage of Colors in Ocean's Brew

Waves swirl colors, a painter's delight,
Every splash sparks laughter, what a sight!
Pufferfish puff up, not quite so tough,
Blowing bubbles, they can't get enough!

Anemones wiggle, wearing a grin,
They tickle the toes of turtles swimming in!
Bright parrotfish chatter, "Is that you, mate?"
"Let's race to the reef, it'll be first-rate!"

Sea turtles crack jokes; their humor's old,
While dolphin flips spark joy uncontrolled!
Crabs do the cha-cha on the warm sand,
While clownfish pull faces, oh isn't it grand?

Even the seaweed gets in on the fun,
Spinning and swirling, it's dance time, run!
Take a dive and join this vibrant crew,
In a colorful world, there's always something new!

Glittering Whispers Beneath the Clouds

Giggles echo in the gentle surf,
As beach balls bounce, what a silly turf!
Shells spin tales of adventures past,
While crabs in shades make each joke last.

A pelican dives with a splash and a flop,
"Is this your best dive?" makes the seabirds stop!
With a wave and a nod, they declare a jest,
"Next time, perhaps, you'll give it your best!"

The tides tickle toes, laughter's their song,
As little fish shimmer, where they belong!
With every wave, a tickle and tease,
The ocean's a comedy, doing as it please!

Seabirds squawk, in a riff on the wind,
Making it clear, this fun's never sinned!
Join the party, where all is bright,
In the watery realm, where laughter takes flight!

Vibrant Flickers in the Briny Blue

Fish in tuxedos dance with glee,
Making waves like a jolly spree.
Crabs with shades, sunbathing right,
Sipping breezes, what a sight!

Jellyfish float with stylish flair,
Waving at turtles, without a care.
Starfish flip like they're on a stage,
Performing tricks, they're all the rage!

Seagulls squawk jokes from high above,
Diving for fries, they're in love.
Ocean bubbles giggle and pop,
Under the waves, the fun won't stop!

In this realm where the silly thrive,
Even the seaweed loves to jive.
With laughter echoing through the spray,
Join in the fun, come splish away!

Light's Serenade Across the Rippling Sea

Waves are whispering tales of jest,
Seashells laughing, feeling blessed.
Clams play cards, oh what a game!
While dolphins race in a frothy fame.

The sun's a clown with a golden grin,
Juggling rays as it dips in.
Octopuses humorously squirt,
Making fish seem a little curt!

A crab punches in, clocking his hours,
At the reef, where the fun devours.
Coral reefs burst with colors bright,
Underwater parties ignite the night!

So come along, let's splash and play,
In this watery world, come what may.
With giggles afloat on every tide,
Join the frolic, let joy be your guide!

Dreamlike Radiance in Nature's Pool

Bubbles dance like giggling sprites,
Splashing joy in sunny heights.
Fish wearing sunglasses swim around,
Fins flipping with the laughter sound.

A turtle joins the playful race,
With a grin upon its face.
Jellyfish twirl in wobbly glee,
Pretending they swim like a bumblebee.

Beacons of Light in Aquatic Tranquility

Lampshades float like charming dreams,
Casting light in watery beams.
Octopuses juggle shiny shells,
Telling secrets that only fish tell.

Crabs play poker with clams galore,
Betting shells and then wanting more.
A dolphin leaps with a silly twist,
Squeaking songs that cannot be missed.

Memories Illuminated in Ocean's Gaze

Coconuts bob on a buoyant spree,
Dancing to a tune from the sea.
Starfish sunbathe, arms held out wide,
Waving hello with glimmering pride.

Seagulls cackle, making a fuss,
Stealing fries with a sneaky gust.
A clam fashion show, pearls on display,
Would make any shellfish shout, 'Hooray!'

Reflections of a Distant Star

Waves giggle, flicking this and that,
Echoing laughter, as pinchers chat.
A mermaid sips her glowing brew,
While a crab breaks dance, it's all quite new.

Sandcastles topple in waves of fun,
As kids dive in, splashing everyone.
The sun sets down with a cheeky grin,
A day well spent, let the laughter begin.

www.ingramcontent.com/pod-product-compliance
Lightning Source LLC
Chambersburg PA
CBHW060145230426
43661CB00003B/581